FiRE

WATCHER

ESSENTIAL POETS SERIES 201

Canada Council
for the Arts

Conseil des Arts
du Canada

Guernica Editions Inc. acknowledges the
support of the Canada Council for the Arts
and the Ontario Arts Council.
The Ontario Arts Council is an agency of the
Government of Ontario.

We acknowledge the financial support of the
Government of Canada through the Canada
Book Fund (CBF) for our
publishing activities.

ONTARIO ARTS COUNCIL
CONSEIL DES ARTS DE L'ONTARIO

50 YEARS OF ONTARIO GOVERNMENT SUPPORT OF THE ARTS
50 ANS DE SOUTIEN DU GOUVERNEMENT DE L'ONTARIO AUX ARTS

Vivian Demuth

FIRE WATCHER

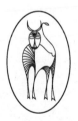

GUERNICA

TORONTO – BUFFALO – BERKELEY – LANCASTER (U.K.)
2013

Michael Mirolla, editor
Elana Wolff, poetry editor
Guernica Editions Inc.
P.O. Box 117, Station P, Toronto (ON), Canada M5S 2S6
2250 Military Road, Tonawanda, N.Y. 14150-6000 U.S.A.

Distributors:
University of Toronto Press Distribution,
5201 Dufferin Street, Toronto (ON), Canada M3H 5T8
Gazelle Book Services, White Cross Mills, High Town, Lancaster
LA1 4XS U.K.

First edition.
Printed in Canada.

Legal Deposit – First Quarter
Library of Congress Catalog Card Number: 2012954448
Library and Archives Canada Cataloguing in Publication

Demuth, Vivian, 1958-
Fire watcher / Vivian Demuth.

(Essential poets series ; 201)
Issued also in electronic formats.
ISBN 978-1-55071-696-2

I. Title. II. Series: Essential poets series ; 201

PS8607.E593F57 2013   C811'.6   C2012-907980-4

For the Rocky Mountain eco-communities
and
for Eliot

CONTENTS

the edge of the receding glacier

where painfully and with wonder
at having survived even
this far

we are learning to make fire

— Margaret Atwood

Writing in the Dark

The generator won't start.
Werewolves crash in the bush.
Drunk wind stumbles in the trees.
Hornets and flies want in,
sometimes I want out.
But not now – when fireweed
turns scarlet, trees are decked in gold.
And silence waits patiently
to see who will make
the first move.

Desolation Devi/l

Nose Mountain Fire Tower – transitory torturer
of a thousand disguises (I wish you'd make up your mind).
You're a nomadic tick on my tush,
supreme outhouse boredom, sitting on your
chameleon throne, endless blue-webbed sites above.
Below, a rug of cumuli – everyone, everything
buried in your grave vapours. I'm your captive
audience – victim of your postmodern horror-show.

You send mists of flying crayfish, harbingers of
things to come. Force me to perform musical chairs –
open/close a cage of windows. You tinkle on my books when
I'm not looking, then the electric chair. Hey, Fire Tower,
What's that tingling on top of my head? Spark after spark.
You're a primitive chain-smoker, I'm not your flint.
That zapping shit freaks me out – Do you know
how much paperwork all that lightning generates?

You know everything. I try to escape your chamber,
you blast me with your wicked breath – gale force
of a hundred klicks per minute. Winds that shake me up,
up in the red/white fibreglass nest. I open the trap,
you slam my head – I grab the grounded ladder
in my underpants. You stimulate the winds,
you howl: *Hypothermia is here*,
Really like dead blue legs, don't you?

Your halitosis smothers me, bombs me in a
barf of hail. I no longer hear the whisper of elves.
You think I'll slip on those icy ball-bearings where
grass once grew, and suffocate.
You puke on my vegetable beds, try to starve me,
know I can take only so many shrivelled morels,
only so much fireweed.

After a pinball of purple storms, you not only send me
one rainbow, but two. Seductress of my heightened
senses, you shred me to pieces. I'm just another slow chew.
You want more of me, bring in the damn fog,
three long days of obscurity.
Every day a novel sound – I've had it.
Stepping over another headless hare.
Keep it to yourself.

O Nose Mountain Fire Tower, you amorous annihilator –
you send shimmering bluebirds, pink bohemian
waxwings that make my binoculars drop,
my falling black eyes – my bruised I.
You want my job, you want it all.
On my birthday, you send barn swallows,
feathered bombers to make my day your day.
You take everything.

After dreaming of sex, I wander among a minefield of
tracks, your ravens on the roof. And you,
disguised as a bear, come to skin my friend's cat.
Thanks for the white guys you send for entertainment.

I yell hello, they leap into the bush like wolves do.
I hope you die laughing. When I'm naked with mosquitoes
taking a solar shower, you send drunk loggers,
knowing I want treehuggers.

Heartless Tower, shame on you and your obnoxious abstinence.
No visitors, nothing for four days, then a family of bears.
A Russian roulette of tag – you make me forget my name.

O Fire Tower, what do you want from me?
I'm seducing someone under your summer night
and you outshine me with your whips of northern lights.
That's it, you really want to fuck me – don't you? –
screw the brains out of me and eat them. Yes – I'd die
a thousand ecstasies with you. Did you hear that
Ranger Bob? 10-4 everything is just fine up here
on plain old Nose Mountain Fire Tower.

The Mountain Fire Tower

Mongrel clouds lift a sad shroud. Grey and brown valleys yield to green. A few furtive songbirds mate among stoic evergreens and a little oven bird cries, "Teacher, teacher." On Nose Mountain, weather instruments stand alone, the white weather station stands alone. The clear rain gauge stands alone and I, like the steel fire tower, stand alone, watching for forest fires while the mountain works on me. But the fire tower is condemned, unstable, dangerous, and I its captive migrant. I scratch my crotch like men do in public, then enter the cedar cabin to a dawn chorus of bombings in the Middle East, nuclear weapons broiling around the cracked globe, women telling their war rape stories. I turn down the heat and wander outside, searching for something to hold onto – the ladder on the fire tower, too cold. See myself as a white-rumped hawk hovering above thinking, no hands. Lingering snowdrifts disappear. The alpine magnetic field surges, crackling wind's larynx. I wonder how not to discipline a spectre. I see and hear purple fairy orchids hidden under spruce. See and hear in between everything I have known. See myself as a white wolf howling, "When will the cities ring free?" The mountain shakes – a muted orgasm – says nothing. It's too soon. I have just arrived. Haven't collapsed into the silence or something naked. But an albino bear appears and grasps the rain gauge with its grinning teeth, dances into the bush while a flock of pink bohemian waxwings flies away with the weather station. "Ah, relative freedom," I shout to the moon's skull peeking out. But I am afraid. Will defiant mountains be destroyed? The mountain has much to say, it cannot all be translated. Will we too disappear?

> In the illuminated darkness
> On a rocky mountain
> Wild shadows
> Eclipse the moon

Hare Poetics

A tan doe,
her white tail
waving goodbye.

Ah loneliness –
come in.
Make yourself at home.

Sunrise
glistening snow tracks:
hare poetics.

Rain dripping
on plastic rain barrel:
shamanic drum.

Grey fog –
month of heavy rain,
I drowned.

In the Middle of the Watershed

I sit on a rogue boulder
    high in alpine fields
        reading Gary Snyder.
My mind in the Rocky Mountains,
    I watch blue glaciers blanketed with toxaphene
        running away from the heat.
I reflect on the silvery river,
    mirror of change, below.
Turn north, eye to the swollen river-sea
    mouth where floating whales blow
        toxic through spouts.
O weaving licentious river,
    all the dirt slides down
        your logged slopes.
I face west, where trout jump through rainbows
    then disappear in silent oil-drilling
        mud-spill.
Eagles circle, eyeing the thirsty waters.
    I turn east, ear on explosive underground
        streams of West Bank water wars.
Man's globe is leaking,
    there are no neutral benedictions.
O mind of filtering bones and eggs
    in sunken foamy pools, I face south,
        with SPF 306 sunblock on skin.
No potions for mutant three-legged frogs.
    Holy dwindling rivers in this multi-mega
        industrial watershed: They're opening up
the country while closing down our ancient minds.

Look: We are the frogs, the whales, the eagles –
 we claim spawnage from ice age flows.
We are the Nobel Laureate trout,
 taking the river to an unmade bed.

VIVIAN DEMUTH

Grouse Dance

Morning mating rouses me,
naked in the cabin bed.
A male blue grouse flares his red
throat pouch to hoot and prance
with a female who struts
away.

I enter the dance
with camera in hand,
to capture the male's fan of
displayed tail feathers.
We dart in circles, leaping
at each other's deepest voice.
How close can I get?

At the last turn,
he cocks his eager eye
and sings, his neck pulsing,
before he seeks another bird.

Holdover

Deep down in the roots,
an ember has been held
from burnt brush piles
of winter explorations
for oil.
Deep inside,
the spark remains.
It glows like an eyeball
until over time
summer's heat and
charged winds
ignite through the roots,
sparks flaring the air
in the blindness of night.
I awake at dawn in your arms
to the summer's largest fire,
clouds of aromatic smoke
emanate from
              inside.

Bush Fire

Below firetower heights,
smoke explodes
in multiple shapes of claws.

I watch fires cross borders,
eye water bombers
like slow vultures,
circle oil fires,
see helicopters with fighters;
a red chemical falls, blood
stains flaming ground.
But nothing stops choking breath,
the burning of bush. Heroic
smoke screen creeps from city
to forests, invades papers – articles
erased.

I want to breathe again.
Let us inspire.

Pitch of wounded white pines
ignites a backfire, sparks an army –
river on left, bare soil on right.
Winged creatures –
furious winds in front.
Fiery sap alights
a bio-community in dark of night.
Firewalls push hissing bush

back to an axis of protective stones.
Through my tower lenses,
fire cleanses down to the ground –
till workers build new frames
and forest litters breed:
roots, bacteria, seedlings,
resurrected doves.

Bears

You have terrorized me in the middle of the road,
followed me for miles forcing me to climb a flimsy
radio tower. Eaten all the dandelions before I could
make them wine. You have seduced me with your
milk chocolate coats and astonished me with monstrous
footprints between my broccoli plants. Aroused me
from time-travel dreams by banging your big noses
on my bedroom window and knocking on the cabin
door uninvited for dinner. Albinos, you're really wild
and telling people about seeing you gets me labelled crazy.
Mothers, you feed me with your parade of fumbling cubs.
Bears, you've taught me how to live uncomfortably,
made me laugh at Death's claws. You're the best damn
company a lone fire watcher can have. But watch out
for beasts like me – we turn up the planetary heat,
disrupt your age-old winter sleep.

Summer

– for Eliot

I wander on Nose Mountain
with cerulean bluebirds
while you groove
in a borough beyond the clouds.
Here a shed moose antler
riddled with your poems.
Your soft eyes winking
in the snowshoe hare,
forever eating angels.
Your nocturnal travails
with long bear claws
shifting on the skin
of my alpine dreams –
my hummingbird flight.
I seek the naked smell
of you in the pines,
pick your old bones
from the big wolf scat
on the road and kiss them
till you and I come
together again.

Nose Mountain Song

From my dreams they are waking me,
waking me.

I am spring without winter,
mother divorced from science.

I am the bear pausing on the road,
from my dreams, wakened.

They are mad trippers burning up the earth;
I am not afraid.

The draggers haul shells from bombed out
dwellings; I outrun them.

They are bewilderers of birds and insects;
I eat all of them.

The reapers seed clouds with dirty tears.
I pray under ancient dark fur.

I am the bear, they are waking me.
We are baring our teeth,

scratching the underground roots.
Poor-sighted, sniffing tracks of alternate

dimensions, lost in lack of habitat.
We are listening for evergreen voices

whispering directions.

Fairy Slipper

An orange butterfly
tenderly probes my toes
till I wake up.

Two horseflies
fucking while flying
away.

I am a pink fairy slipper
waiting to be
cross-pollinated.

Lightning crashing
all around –
illuminated brain.

Violet storms
and fire watchers
crack like radio waves.

Ghost

Loud, like two men yelling in unknown tongues.
You dragged your feet in the midnight cupola.
I went for the forestry radio,
froze –
a cornered rabbit below.
Nights you shuffled across the floor,
sank slowly in my creaky chair.
I tossed and turned till I couldn't stand it.
                    Phantom,
I picked stones and prayed –
placed them around the lookout – "Go away."
One week later, freakish storms
of sexual dreams and daytime foreplay
hinted at your presence again.
                        But soon I left for winter
wanderings; perhaps you found another warm soul
        for company.

VIVIAN DEMUTH

Song of the Uncommon Snipe

I'm awakened at dawn
by an incessant call from outside.
A cosmopolitan snipe in the sky
dives overhead for a mate.
His body elicits a winnowing,
"Youououououou," louder than all
the chanting songbirds and crows.
Near a damp meadow, I arrange
a few scraps of grass in my bed
and listen to the snipe's gregarious call.
I fall into bed, thinking, "Alright, take me,"
and sigh: "Youououououou."

Tree Talk

A big black bear and two cubs
had hung around the fire tower a week
      feeding on fiery red bearberries.
One morning the mountain exhaled a breeze.
Dandelions opened, ecstatic in sunshine.
One cub nuzzled her mother's fur
      shiny in the northern, salmon sun.
The other cub, with white-patch forehead,
      nipped its sibling's tiny feet.
I decided to bring out my grizzly bear skull,
a gift given me by a park warden
      after a female had died from a
      dart that punctured her gut.
With bear skull in my lap, I sat down
      on my cabin porch.
Suddenly, the pine tree I was looking at
      started shaking furiously,
the only tree of hundreds in the yard
      moving at all.
The mother bear approached and rose up
      tall on her great hind legs,
      staring at the single shaking tree;
I watched transfixed
      from the porch,
      bear skull in hand.
Who said bears have poor eyesight?
When the one-tree tempest stopped
      just as suddenly
      as it began,

mother bear fell to the ground
      feasting on bearberries again, sniffing
       in the direction of my breathlessness.
Later I placed my bear skull
      into that big old tree.
The bear and I –
      we rise like a windstorm
      from deep hibernations
to witness these old trees talk.

Green Curtains

Full moon breathing
on this incandescent stage,
coming and going.

Magic theatre of stars
reveals a story
no one on Broadway can see.

3 a.m. fall skies
rouse me for a performance:
neon northern lights.

Evenings I sing of the earth –
green curtains of aurora borealis
draw closer.

Ah loneliness –
start packing your bags.
Soon the tower will close.

Woman in Green 1

Green, it's your green I love.
— Federico García Lorca

Her first day on the job, male park rangers
turn greener than their uniforms,
froth at the mouth, chant 10-codes, 10-4.
      Think she's deer-like –

with ungulate eyes, bionic ears, twitching
nose, hushed strut in a spruce-green suit.
As the spring hunt sounds its first
      blue moonless night,

the green men beat her with rabid flashlights,
stroke her ribs and tits with pitons. Her breasts
slip away, heart climbs upslope. Body,
      shocked and pawed,

is thrown to a grizzly, near dead in a trap.
But that's not who she is. The wind whistles:
Teach your toes to turn into claws. Recollect.
      The bear undresses,

gives her his coat for the cold, succumbs in her
humming arms. She remembers something old as
she strokes his broken bones. She rips off her
      tattered uniform, takes

his penis inside her, feels her breasts re-grow,
antennae nipples. Before dying, the bear
bites off his penis, gives it to her. She creeps
       home adorned in the bear's

coat. At dawn she dons a sharp new tie, fresh
uniform and comes in late. The rangers crack
jokes, offer her their venison lunch. She
       takes a bite,

then shares with them her carved toothpick.
They pick, not knowing, it's the bear's prick.
She takes notes and her heart begins
       to soften.

Woman in Green 2

Woman in green, she loves conversant mountains.
Lipstick gone, she kisses queer glacial lakes,
releases rainbow trout from her split lip.
       The fish speak to her

of kidnap, slippery poachers she will surprise.
She trusts fish who envelop her in alluvial rings.
As her fish-tail grows, drunken mountains cry.
       Crevasses warm

and she drips desire, touches glaciers
edging off park maps. On backcountry
ski patrols she digs a snow pit.
       These crystals, she says,

portend release. She warns the male rangers,
their laughter triggers an avalanche,
its fingers tuck the park offices in
       sleepy debris.

In cold wind, an old bear eyes her, dragging
frozen tongues behind. Owls screech.
With flagging tape, she guides lost
       souls out of the park.

Woman in Green 3

Woman in green vacuums the lime sprayed
on dirt roads so fir trees can cross safely,
sings to porcupines who respond
         with raucous love.

She hides earwigs in mountaineers' ears with
geographical precision, protects the earwigs
from scientists' fiscal desires dressed up
         in lab coats and park acts.

She cradles fallen male mountaineers in a metal
basket that she flies to muttering rangers – men
hate being rescued by her. Male rangers
         pose for the news.

The blood of wounded climbers stains her boots.
She squats to pee to clean them while the rangers
watch in contempt. Forest breezes massage
         the pages of her skin.

Woman in Green 4

Woman in green patrols the traffic of stars
to illuminate unpaved trails for lost cougars.
She resuscitates water lilies whose eyes
           tear from city smog.

After debriefings, she deletes "man" in "man hours"
on rescue forms, tourniquets the veins of a
gold mine to help it sleep beneath
           the clamour of men.

She sets radio-collared bears free on new roads.
Hikers hear the buzz of her chainsaw, read
signs that warn against eating lake fish,
           wonder where the wilderness

ran. At night by a whining grove of logged trees,
the wind takes her uniform. She replants
clear-cuts with Jack pines and marmots who
           whistle stories again.

Woman in Green 5

On her last day in green, a rock slide
drums the alarm. A logger's bank of evergreens
turns red, then loses its needles. The earth spirits who
        sent her to infiltrate

summon her back. She enters the mouth of the
underground mountain, adds her uniform
to a pot of skulls, reads a recipe
        from her patrol notes,

boils a soup of warmed bats. The green men
will die of heat. There's no delight in stressed death.
She feeds the earth a cool metre, then
        burns the human waste.

Oh women, if you are lost in neon valleys
thirsting for sundew dreams, or stuck on slopes with
cold men, call her: "Woman in Green" –
        she will return.

Dear Wilderness Women Officers

We are waiting for you in the rainbowed ecotone, the wild zone in between black and white that you have researched but never found, bound in your uniforms.

Perhaps you are stoic superwomen, but when you feel the impact of abiocoens in your environmental assessments, azoic in your chest desiring a thigmotropic response, then disrobe and carry your detritus to the backside of a report, or lie.

Consider entering these cadenced climes. We will wait for you at the cliff edge, where we will feed you devil's root to talk with the wind and run with the trees before you leap.

But the sun is ticking. Hurry before the uniform handcuffs your aortic eye forever. Your badge is killing you alive. Reach for the hand in the spider's web. Your real name drips in the sap of trees. Hurry before your stars fall sleepy with fatigue. We keep vegetal narratives lit for fireflies like you.

Wilderness Climbs, A Woman's Guide

If you've registered with a Human Rights Commission
for work discrimination, you might contemplate the windswept
sky, pray as you near your wilderness route.
At the base of your solo climb, stretch your sore eyes,
converse with the rough mountain, even if it doesn't
seem to respond. You'll need help from all quarky dimensions.
Wrap nylon stockings around the bulge of the first pitch:
And whereas
> *for her examination*
>> *of the policy on harassment …*

And whereas
> *the complainant*
>> *qualifies …*

Watch your balance. At this point in the climb you may desire
redress of the entire Act. Instead, remove some steamy clothing.
Drink plenty of water. Jam your hands into the damp shadows.
Remember to boldly place bolts and screws from your rack
into sacred cracks for cyborgs and future women to clip into.
And if you can't get good handholds, insert wired hexes and
steel friends in the gaps before deleting the tricky pitch:
Now therefore
> *the parties*
>> *agree …*

Caution: Do not party at this altitude. You may lose focus,
fall onto mad rock.

It is under-
        stood ...

your skin will crack and bleed. No moleskin will suffice.
But if you lick your body, you may conjure love. And in a few
years, your muscles will repair. For now, hug not the rock.
Watch instead for turds and smiling snakes in the outcroppings
of:
It is agreed ...

This a good place to rest, eat chocolate. You may lose
your appetite, hear backbiting voices yell from above:
Who needs a woman ahead of her time?
But glance down, see how far your body
has climbed. Listen to the rock's pulse,
wind lifting your backpack. Prepare your
Self for the dark chimney of:
Settlement agreements
                without prejudice ...

You may require diamond cams or super nuts for gnarled
wisecracks. If you slip, advocates and lawyers may try
to catch you, still you'll bruise. There's no relief but instant
medicine – bitter arnica growing in crevices.
Remember: No climb is ever perfect. Near the end, at:
Satisfaction of action
        employment of women and visible minorities
                arising ...

delight in the poetry of toe-jam.
And at the final mossy overhang of :

                              Dated at …

                                    pursuant to …

your body will surely ache.
Yet as you lift yourself onto the barren peak,
your mind will gasp at the alpine
sight of other women, bears, toadflax,
and earwigs, waving from the stone below.
Your thoughts will be

                        discharged …

                             whereupon

                                  whereto now?

Ice Climbing

Climbing, feet edge on rocky toe-hold,
I poke my head through a moonlit
hole, rest on both sides.

We overnight on a mountain ledge,
dream we're ants driving
tiny cars below.

A steep pitch triggers sewing-machine leg.
My trembling appendage stitches a hidden wound,
eyes and hands reach for the next scarred face.

I haul a rack of weighty technologies,
backpack of granite emergencies;
sling rope to tie into the rock's story.

Ice climbing, I kick crampons, axes
into the frozen waterfall –
lips bleeding water.

I Have Been Calling Them

For a long time   I have been calling them   without reply.
I smell them in the DNA hills of my boreal bed
I see them waiting on a black forest coat of male arms
I hear them arguing, tongues flying in Native winds
I rub their dark feathers dipped in a dry Alberta stream
As I write in the rocky darkness to talk with them.

For a long time   I have been calling them   without response.
And after I saw the twirling Precision helicopter crash
After I ran downhill into the smell of crushed metal and
          dreams
After I touched a cold firefighter's blue-winged lips
with the erratic cry of my breath, then I called them again
while walking alone in logged woods and for once
sixteen ravens landed, then croaked and croaked, lifting me
as we listened to our breath alight in tall evergreens.

Faders

– for Anna Politkovskaya

What fades?
Evergreens, survivors of chain-linked
generations of logging, now a cemetery
of vertical bones with marrow devoured
by defrosted mobs of mountain beetles.
Dry pine trees, fragile, faded red
like splattered blood of hunted journalists
marked in blinding daylight of corruption
and wars. The paper dollar skin of a million
carved trees changes hands to kill or save
a forest, to pay the salary of a determined
investigative reporter or to complete
the handshake of a prearranged hit.
When the deal is done, baked winds
blow tinder needles into the world's circular
currents where the sad news is read by ever-
globalizing children scavenging through
trashed newspapers. This is the hazardous
graveyard, dumped skeletons of trees and
journalists, the unpredictable resting place
from which a thoughtful spark has potential,
in spite of death, to melt and release
a thousand tender seedlings.

Healers

I'm surrounded by families of healers.
Gold arnica flowers in mountain fields –
    masseurs of sore limbs.
Blue juniper berries and fuchsia fireweed –
    cleansers and peppery
    colour in my salad.
Flocks of white yarrow flowers –
    thank you for conversations
    over tea and group meditations.
Blue delphiniums – toxic to lips,
    but purple with trumpets
    that blow nth dimension songs.
Who needs angels when I'm a madwoman
    soothed by looking at you.

After Poetry on the Peaks

After an afternoon flash of human poetry at Poetry on the Peaks near Nose Mountain Fire Tower, I return chairs to engine shed while mosquitoes watch. Wind whistles in the willow and bees buzz the fireweed, long-time mellow friends. The crushed grass, sign of the human party, rises under evening showers. But I'm still charged with a surge of energy from a flock of poets chanting earlier on the ridge. I sleep restlessly and wake unusually early. Inner voice whispers get up. I check on cat. Lured by full moon, I search the morning sky. From radio-room window, I see a mule deer eating beneath firetower scaffolding. A string of Tibetan prayer flags flutters on the tower above his head. He lifts his antlers into the rainbow of prayer flags, fireweed leaves dangling from his mouth. Shakes his head, tearing the flags from the tower, and walks away. A draped deer. I wonder if I'm dreaming as he struts into the trees with the colourful flags flowing from his rack.

Kakwa River Under Full Moon

Stay away from the Kakwa River when the moon is full.
Footloose predators sharpen their teeth in the trembling foliage.
Buried pack horses and broken airplanes rise from the glowing
hills. Somewhere a forest is burning. The orange-smoked face
of that unobstructed moonlight sends rabid wolves running
from water. Even the hot shadows of spruce trees cannot stand
still. Such blistering haunting. But if your lips are parched, your
weary body burning, and you can stand the brilliant torture of a
starless sky, then cozy up to thirsty stones drinking at the Kakwa
gravel bar. Splash the wild horses blowing steamy snorts, holler
like a rainbow trout and drink the river's sweet salmon radiance.
Forget all rhyme and reason till your dry, sore throat can sing
again – alive as a heavenly ghost. If you get lost, I'll find you in
this moonlit river, imbibing in these gilded hills. Your lips, your
tongue, your longing, quenched in this waterfall-light.

Kananaskis

Your cool skin seemed a challenge
to touch at that alpine height and angle.
I stepped cautiously in Swiss mountain
boots on your tongue of steep snow. By ranger
radio, I pronounced I was crossing over, completing
a loop. A rock tumbled, trumpeting in the valley. You
froze as Time held its breath. My toes stretched to listen –

Not that way, you whispered. I stopped. You slapped
me with an exhale of wind. Not that way. I abandoned
your snowy face to pick my way slowly down your rocky
hip. Stones slipped beneath me, rolling hundreds of feet below.
I held onto rocks, felt for a hidden map, followed your lead –

You pulled clouds off the sun. Hot and damp, I finally sensed
your soft meadow underfoot. I flung off my pack, peeled off
my ranger shirt, rolled in your tiny blue ankles of alpine forget-
me-nots, stroked your green toes and yelled to the valley –
    We are God.

Post-Meditation

I was cooking rhubarb.
Eliot was talking
Ginsbergian mind drifts
while washing dishes –
shared labour
in the alpine cabin's
flying fog.
The cat murmured in his dreams.
Mindful moments streamed
like shifting mists,
as big blue heavens rested
above the vapours
waiting for uplift –
or just being
sky.

Home with Wolves

I was a wolf once, on one September day of thousands.
Two wolves were waiting on the mountain road. I howled,
badly, inviting them to lookout cabin like a wistful sister
        should.
Four of their relatives heard, jumped out of the bush and joined
the party like a community would. I watched enchanted
as six wolves laughed and trotted the icy road toward me –
cha-chung, cha-chung, cha-chung, ha, ha, ha.
I ran inside for my camera to capture the revelry.
Erratic, stumbling through the door, I returned
to the road rippling with wolves,
but they knew first that my wolf-self was gone.
They leapt into the bush complaining, sniffing the ground,
while I was left panting – ha, ha, ha – pacing around,
waiting for my excited wolfishness to be found.

The Age of Extinction

A few nights ago, a bear danced around my garden carrots
       and bowed to sniff the sow's scat in the soil bed.
Last summer, a deer yanked my Tibetan prayer flags
      from fire-tower scaffolding
and paraded adorned antlers past trampled skulls
       in the broken forest.
I'm a human animal walking a dirt trail of illusions,
       tossing vegetable scraps a mile from cabin
       for the closest or quickest to snack.
In my first six years of alpine-solitude wrestling,
       I saw a hungry caribou outrun
       a wild six-pack of dart-gun helicopters,
heard ravens chuckle circling above loggers'
       orange flagging tape alit in forest flames,
followed a scarred moose chase a fleeing Honda generator
       along another new mountain road,
and took photos of a wolf pack stealing the seismic camp's
       grilling steaks and biting off a page
       from the First Handbook of Habitat Protection.
Over the next six years from mountain heights, I've watched
       the wildlife thin and the oil drills strike back.
Is this the Age of Extinction in which only Fortune's wheels
       will roll on?
I pray that some drugged grizzly will wake up
       and flip the switch.
Can a human ever gain the insight of a drugged bear?
In the meantime, I'll sit in the petrified bedrock
       with what looks like a young dinosaur
       and write for the unwritten record.

Animal Conscience

I was having one of my monthly anthropomorphic dreams
        when a finch
called from the tallest spruce, I'm a precocious bird and this
        I've heard:
Animals fancy pleasure. I've seen bears toboggan up and down
        spring
slopes. As with you, animal intelligence varies. A
        compassionate polar
bear in the Vancouver zoo rescued and protected a discarded
        kitten.
Teams of dolphins have saved two-legged surfers from shark's
        jaws.
Elephants sing over the bones of their dead. Even Conservation
        Officers
have witnessed mother bears cry – grieving after poachers
        killed their cubs.

Our animal conscience seems arcane to you? How shall I trill
so you will not chafe outright? My little body can shout you
a sonnet and trample you in a game of solitude. Can you travel
without money and eat your failed ambitions? Can you kiss the
gleam in my flighty eye? I disdain arrows. Let us sing
        covenants,
of avian respect. O tender humans, restring your faunal
        instruments.

Rufous

There's a hummingbird
                    in my throat

I can't stop
                    sipping
                              the sparkling wine
of her buzz
                    I'm coloured with
                                        rufous indulgence

When feeding
                    I hover above
                              the iridescence
                                        of her light

I'm not pugnacious
                    doctors   it's just important
                                        to realize
that fields full of
                    old hummers
                              are not safely
                                        identified

Their wing-beats
                    so rapid   blur
                                        mindstreams
                                        drum chants

Sparrow

While doing dishes I heard you crying, an abandoned
baby. I lifted you in cupped hand hoping not to squash
your tiny legs. We searched all corners of the mountain
looking for parents or a kind relative. You were fashionably
grey with chestnut eyebrows, wings too young to fly.
Finally I heard another sparrow in some willow and placed
you nearby. Minutes later you were still alone, and in death's
grip. I massaged your heart, fed you mosquitoes and set you
on my chest at night. In the morning, I found you content
in my feather bed. What is it in nature that leaves
an innocent, lone and weeping, and gives a group
of predators enough deer and beer to party in groups
of thirty or more? After returning you to health, I sent
you off to your wild home. Now I wonder who's
watching me out there? When I look in the mirror
at my hazel eyes and greying hair, I see vestiges
of feathers that will fly around the dawn of flaming
rigs and clear-cuts, till death clips all our wings.

Fire Watcher

– for Stephanie Stewart

We never thought our fire towers would be sites of confusion
like Babel in the Bible, till a seventy-year-old lookout woman
disappeared from her pretty tower of fire.

I've been chased by bears, seen choppers crash, but the worst
nightmare of all is not knowing what happened to Stephanie
at her pristine tower of fire.

We keep an eye out for her kidnapper, honour her
as we look through our scopes, pray no more women
disappear at these steely towers.

The government tells us to beware,
talks of putting up a fence,
but we are meditators who refuse to be caged.

And now, with panic buttons in place, we might jump
when ravens shriek, but we are mourners who refuse to leave
the trees at our desolate towers of fire.

Chicken Creek Area From Copton Ridge

To sit writing impressionistic lines on the electromagnetic stage of copper-iron rocks on a muted summer day is to confess to creeks, but not chickens hiding in verbs of vermillion pack-trails, or lighter deciduous adverbs that leak dark urgencies of a territory carved by straight lines, not of ochre strokes bandaging blue hills with hidden roads at a bearish horizon below long vowels of light interrupted by muddy nouns sliding on grey shores of sky, not sobbing onto sentences of forest sculpting a play of designs – an umber Native burial ground, for example, that is not hungry for silver phrases from glossy archives.

Live Earth

The concert goers gather where the earth is slanted,
   sheltered from city lights –
where the land still grows verdant words,
   not slick pavement and glowing machines
   who fear and suffocate poems.
The wandering moon fills their refugee mouths.
The homeless wind sprinkles a rouge of cosmic
   dust on their skins to magnetize their memories.
An orphaned grizzly cub taps his claw three times
   on a fire-tower woman's arthritic shoulders.
Gray wolves lick Cree words hidden beneath buffalo horns.
There are no police with their song and dance –
   that's for the birds who punctuate the budding
   text from their nests and cover any half-naked chicks.
Pine beetles spit three times at the evergreens who cough
   and remind all that the word "pristine"
   died invisibly in the grey rain long ago.
Shadow dinosaurs roar three times, then give up their fossils.
And as a tired sun rises, it sears the text onto the soiled
   bodies of the gathered.
The fire-tower woman feels the marks in the moist forest
   between her toes – three short, three long, three short.
Ask her along the game trail and she will reveal the boreal
   understory – a rhizomatic SOS.

Black Hole

I watch the alpine night
vibrating with blinking stars
that collapse like us
in a warped, hazy galaxy,
inner and outer pressures
unable to withstand
our shining shapes
and atomic instabilities.
Explosive energies
blast ancestral designs and
bleating hearts into black holes
as we cross borders
in hellish heat.
Orion watches our destruction
among specks of dust
in the dark aerial desert,
while our cosmic citizenship
burns in the big bang
of another abstract war.
Alone on an illuminated mountain,
I sit under the wings of
Pegasus, watching as new constellations
and dreamscapes are born.

Indian Graves Near Grande Cache, Moonlight

The leaning crosses have no shadows. Iridescent magenta, blue night sky makes spirit wander. The tall and leafless tree has seen it all. First Nations and buffalo coming and going, poised as the full and empty moon. Warm greys, dappled pinks, a paradise to die for. Snow-peaks mimic wood-frame forms of silvered spirit houses. Is anybody home? Dark gaps peer through slatted walls. Humans and non-humans intermingle like cached ancestral lovers, talking in acrylic dreams. Cloaked in sparkle-snow, the moonlit voices kiss the land. Beauty seeking its own.

Buddha Bar

At the Buddha Bar just around the corner from Starbucks,
some people drink in the shadows while others stand looking
toward the lights as if to be beamed up. Some stand on their
heads because they're tired of sitting, but no one minds at the
Buddha Bar where buddhas and dakinis chuckle at the big
screen featuring endless G.I. Joe wars. I like to sip on a kindly
wine and watch monks and nuns recite the Fire Sermon from
a tightrope strung above. They stir fear while I ride the burning
neurons of my mind, until I quietly burp – Ah, nothing but air –
and wait for the next poem, and freedom from suffering for all.

NOTES

Desolation Devi/l
"Devi" is a Hindi word for goddess.

Ghost
This poem was written at Copton fire lookout, which is built differently than fire towers, in that it is a two-floor structure with the lookout cupola on the second floor above the living quarters.

I Have Been Calling Them
Darcy Moses was a Cree firefighter from Sturgeon Lake, Alberta, who died tragically in a helicopter crash at Nose Mountain fire tower in July 2006, while fighting forest fires. His mother, Margaret, and her family have visited the memorial created for her son on Nose Mountain.

Faders
Anna Politkovskaya was a Russian investigative journalist who was murdered in Moscow in 2006. Faders is a Forestry term for pine trees that have been infested by pine beetles.

Kakwa River Under Full Moon
A reproduction of this acrylic painting can be found in: *Trail North: A Journey in Words and Pictures* (1995), by Bob Guest. "Kakwa" is a Cree word for porcupine. The Kakwa River and Nose Mountain are located in the Smoky Watershed.

Kananaskis
Kananaskis is the Cree name of an aboriginal man who, as legend has it, survived an axe blow to the head. It was also the name of a Provincial Park in Alberta.

Fire Watcher
In August 2006, fire lookout Stephanie Stewart went missing while working at Athabasca fire tower near Hinton, Alberta. She has never been found.

Chicken Creek Area From Copton Ridge
A reproduction of this acrylic painting can be found in: *Trail North: A Journey in Words and Pictures* (1995), by Bob Guest. A forestry fire lookout is located on Copton Ridge.

Indian Graves Near Grande Cache, Moonlight
A reproduction of this acrylic painting by Alberta artist Bob Guest can be found in the journal, *Wild Lands Advocate,* issue 2008-12, Vol.16, No. 6.

ACKNOWLEDGEMENTS

Thanks to my publishers, Michael Mirolla and Connie McParland, for their support, and to my editor, Elana Wolff, for her thoughtfulness and editorial suggestions. I would like to acknowledge the Aseniwuche Winewak Nation, and the Stoney First Nation, on whose territories I have lived and worked for many years. I would also like to acknowledge, with love and gratitude, the Nose Mountain community in the Smoky watershed, the Forestry staff, many friends who have given me their support, and especially my partner, Eliot Katz.

Grateful acknowledgement is made to the editors of publications in which these poems, some in earlier versions, have appeared:

In anthologies: "Live Earth" in *Writing the Land,* eds. Dymphny Dronyk and Angela Kublik, Edmonton, Canada: Blue Skies Press, 2007; "Home With Wolves" in *Home and Away*, eds. Dymphny Dronyk and Angela Kublik, Edmonton, Canada: Blue Skies Press, 2009; "Desolation Devi/l" in *Nose Mountain Moods*, ed. Elroy Deimert, Grande Prairie, Alberta: Smoky Peace Press, 2002.

In journals: "Holdover," and "Black Hole," in *Napalm Health Spa*; "Desolation Devi/l" in *Long Shot;* "The Mountain Fire Tower" in *Hobo Camp Review*; "Kananaskis" in *Reflections*; "Tree Talk" in *Tree Magic*; "Faders" in *Political Affairs*; "In the Middle of the Watershed" in *The Prairie Journal*; "Fairy Slipper" in *Proteus*; "Summer" in *Promethean*; "I Have Been Calling Them" in The League of Canadian Poets blog; "Woman in Green #1," and "Woman in Green #3," in *The Goose*; "Wilderness Climbs, A Woman's Guide," in *Room*.

ABOUT THE AUTHOR

Vivian Demuth is the author of a novel, *Eyes of the Forest* (Smoky Peace Press, 2007), and a poetry chapbook, *Breathing Nose Mountain* (Long Shot, 2004). Her work has appeared in journals and anthologies in Canada, Europe, Mexico, and the United States. She has worked as a park ranger and park warden, an outdoor educator, and as a fire lookout in the Rocky Mountains, where she hosts an annual Poetry on the Peaks event.

Printed in February 2013
by Gauvin Press,
Gatineau, Québec